A
WHITE
FUNNEL
ALBUM

A WHITE FUNNEL ALBUM

CHRIS COLLARD

TEMPUS

Frontispiece: *Lady Moyra* at Ilfracombe in the late 1920s. (H.G. Owen)

First published 2008

Tempus Publishing
Cirencester Road, Chalford,
Stroud, Gloucestershire, GL6 8PE
www.thehistorypress.co.uk

Tempus Publishing is an imprint of The History Press

British Library Cataloguing in Publication Data.
A catalogue record for this book is available from the British Library.

ISBN 978 0 7524 4698 1

Typesetting and origination by The History Press
Printed in Great Britain

Contents

Other Tempus books by Chris Collard

Acknowledgements

The photographs in this book are taken from my own collection, that of my late friend, Mr H.G. (George) Owen, and those friends and correspondents acknowledged below. Its compilation has given me the opportunity to bring to light many photographs which not only have never been published, but which also have rarely been seen.

The White Funnel Fleet of P. & A. Campbell Ltd was the mainstay of Bristol Channel steamer excursions, but the company's long association with the south coast of England was an integral part of its success. This volume covers both areas.

The book has also given me the opportunity to incorporate a certain amount of what might be called 'White Funnel Trivia' – some details of a more domestic nature which have not been included in my six volumes of the company's history, but which nevertheless form an essential part of its operations.

I wish to express my sincere thanks to all those people who, over the years, have contributed, directly or indirectly, to my researches into paddle steamer history: Dr Donald Anderson, Revd Norman Bird, John Brewer, John Brown, Richard Clammer, Nigel Coombes, Andrew Gladwell, Ken Jenkins, William Lind, Stephen Phillips, John Reypert, Sydney Robinson, Peter Southcombe, Mike Tedstone, Phillip Tolley, Lionel Vaughan and Alan Wakeman.

Also, the late H.A. Allen, Howard Davis, Ernest Dumbleton, Graham Farr, Alfred Harvey, Cyril Hawkins Garrington, John Graham, Jim Hendry, Edwin Keen, Victor Keen, Graham Langmuir, Ernest Nurse, George Owen, Eric Payne, Fred Plant, Dr R.V.C. Richards, Capt. L.G.A. Thomas, Ernest Tucker, Will Widden and Howard Woodberry.

A final word concerning the photographs. Those of known origin are credited accordingly, but in some cases it has been impossible, despite every effort, to establish the identity of the photographers. I must express my apologies if any copyright has been inadvertently infringed and hope that this 'omnibus' acknowledgement will serve as an appreciation of all those people, in recognition of their work and their invaluable contribution to this book.

I have also included a number of snapshot photographs taken by holidaymakers with 'Box Brownie'-type cameras. The quality of their results is somewhat lacking in comparison with the expertise and superior equipment used by the more professional photographers, but nevertheless, their interest value outweighs their quality, and reflects a desire to immortalise happy memories of their summer holidays.

WHITE FUNNEL FLEET

Sailings from

NEWHAVEN

HARBOUR

By **P.S.**

"GLEN GOWER"

(Weather and circumstances permitting)

9.15 a.m.   **TUESDAY, JULY 20th**   Return Fare **4/-**

Circular Trip to **BRIGHTON**

(Returning by Train or Southdown Bus)

9.30 a.m.   **WEDNESDAY, JULY 21**   Return Fare **38/6**

Special Day Excursion to **BOULOGNE**

||| PASSPORTS ESSENTIAL |||

(4 hours ashore.)   Leave Boulogne 6 p.m.   Back at 10.45 p.m.

Tickets obtainable in advance from J. H. BULL & Co., West Quay

---

9.00 a.m.   **THURSDAY, JULY 22nd**   Return Fare **4/-**

Circular trip to **BRIGHTON**

(Returning by Train or Southdown Bus.)

9.15 a.m.   **SUNDAY, JULY 25th**   Return Fare **4/-**

Circular Trip to **BRIGHTON**

(Returning by Train or Southdown Bus.)

9.30 a.m.   **WEDNESDAY, JULY 28**   Return Fare **38/6**

Special Day Excursion to **BOULOGNE**

||| PASSPORTS ESSENTIAL |||

(4 hours ashore.)   Leave Boulogne 6 p.m.   Back at 10.45 p.m.

Tickets obtainable in advance from J. H. BULL & Co., West Quay.

TICKETS TO BE BOOKED ON STEAMER (Children over 3 and under 14 years, half fare)

On trips marked thus, passengers may return to Newhaven by Train or Southdown Bus if they so desire.

Passengers enter Newhaven Harbour at South Police Box, Harbour Station. ⌐(*P.T.O.*)

Hastings Printing Co., Portland Place, Hastings. Telephone: 2450.

A timetable from 1937.

one

The Beautiful Sisters

Early in 1905, John Brown's yard at Clydebank launched two sister ships within four weeks of each other. They had been ordered by the Barry Railway Company and were magnificent examples of the shipbuilder's art. Both the *Gwalia* and *Devonia* were destined for long and eventful careers which would end in tragedy, made all the more poignant by the fact that they were such favourites with the travelling public. They both became White Funnel steamers, plying routes on the South Coast and in the Bristol Channel, as well as serving their country in both world wars. Strangely, they were not popular with some of the Campbell employees – since as they had not been built for the company, they were regarded as not 'ours' – but to the majority they were always known as 'The Beautiful Sisters'.

GWALIA / LADY MOYRA / BRIGHTON QUEEN (1905)

In her Barry Railway days the *Gwalia* steams down Sea Mills Reach in the River Avon, 1906.

Above and opposite below: In 1910 the *Gwalia* was purchased by the Furness Railway and renamed *Lady Moyra,* after the wife of Lord Richard Cavendish, one of the company's directors. She acted as consort to the *Lady Evelyn* on the Barrow to Fleetwood service as well as undertaking longer coastal cruises and excursions. She is seen here approaching Barrow in Furness and, opposite above, at Menai Bridge.

Lady Moyra at anchor in Portland harbour during the First World War. She served as a minesweeper as part of the 17th Fast Sweeping Flotilla which swept the busy English Channel shipping lanes.

Above: Lady Moyra leaving Ilfracombe in 1921. Like the *Lady Evelyn,* in 1919 the *Lady Moyra* joined the Cardiff-based Yellow Funnel Fleet of W.H. Tucker & Co. Ltd in the Bristol Channel, and, as in her Barry Railway days, became a thorn in the side of P. & A. Campbell Ltd. However, Tuckers made little financial headway against the superiority of the White Funnel Fleet and went into liquidation in October 1921. The *Lady Moyra* was purchased by P. & A. Campbell Ltd on 3 August 1922 and re-entered service during the following season.

Passengers landing from the *Lady Moyra,* at anchor off Lynmouth in the late 1920s.

Opposite below: Lady Moyra leaving Ilfracombe in 1923. For a few days after her entry into service in 1923, *Lady Moyra* was commanded by Capt. Peter Campbell. He wanted to see how well the new acquisition performed by running her 'flat out' on a down-Channel trip. He called the firemen together and promised them that if they maintained a full head of steam all the way to Ilfracombe he would pay them a bonus of 10s each on arrival – a considerable sum of money in 1923. This they duly did, and as Peter fulfilled his promise he urged them not to spend it on drink during the few hours that they had ashore before the return trip. Unfortunately, Peter's words fell upon deaf ears. The firemen disappeared into the nearest hostelry and within a very short time were utterly incapable, beyond any hope of 'sobering up' by sailing time. However, with the help of Campbell's Ilfracombe agent, Fred Birmingham, word was passed around the town and a small team of willing and experienced hands was assembled in time to fire the *Lady Moyra's* furnaces for the return trip.

With the *Ravenswood* moored on her port side, the *Lady Moyra* awaits her passengers at Ilfracombe Pier in August 1928. Note that the lifebelt on her paddle box shows her port of registry as Barrow – a legacy of her Furness Railway days. She was re-registered in Bristol in 1933.
(H.G. Owen)

The *Lady Moyra* making her way up the River Tawe to berth at Pockett's Wharf, Swansea, in 1929. (H.G. Owen) From 1923 to 1925 the *Lady Moyra* worked principally on the down–Channel sailings from Cardiff. Because of her somewhat heavy fuel consumption she was laid up in Bristol for the whole of the 1926 season, owing to the miners' strike and consequent shortage of coal. She resumed sailing on 3 June 1927, when she arrived at Swansea for the first time, in place of the *Glen Gower*. This was to be her station for six years, during which time she greatly endeared herself to the people of Swansea and became something of an institution in the town.

Lady Moyra leaving Pockett's Wharf, Swansea, in the late 1920s.

Having cleared the west breakwater, the *Lady Moyra* reaches full speed to cross Swansea Bay, bound for Mumbles and Ilfracombe.

Above and below: Lady Moyra arriving at Ilfracombe in 1929. (H.G. Owen)

Top: Lady Moyra making her way to her anchorage in The Range, off Ilfracombe, in 1929. (H.G. Owen)

Centre: Lady Moyra arriving at Weston in 1929. She has just spent a few hours at anchor offshore during the low water period, and is about to berth at Birnbeck Pier to return her day trip passengers to Minehead and Swansea. (H.G. Owen)

Left: Lady Moyra arriving at Ilfracombe on a rough day in the late 1920s. The exposed Swansea to Ilfracombe crossing was frequently accomplished in very rough seas. On Saturday 23 August 1930, conditions were so exceptional that despite being slowed down to half speed off the Scarweather Lightvessel, she was forced to put back into Swansea after heavy seas smashed two of her after saloon windows and caused other, sundry deck damage.

The *Lady Moyra's* large, after saloon windows had always been particularly vulnerable, and in the winter of 1930/1931 they were reduced in size, as seen in this view of her leaving Ilfracombe in 1931. (H.G. Owen)

The *Lady Moyra* approaching the Victoria Pier, Tenby, in August 1931. (Edwin Keen)

In 1933 the *Lady Moyra* was renamed *Brighton Queen* and changed places with the *Devonia* on the south coast. She is seen here arriving at Brighton for the first time. The memorandum book records:

Tuesday 30 May: *Brighton Queen*, (Capt. W.A. Couves), Cardiff and Penarth to Ilfracombe and Brighton. Dep. 11.48 a.m. with 123 passengers.
Wednesday 31 May: *Brighton Queen*. Arrived Palace Pier, Brighton, 11.38 a.m. Steaming time 23 hours, 29 minutes. 365 miles. Average speed 15.4 knots.

Throughout her Furness Railway career and up until 1932 in her years with White Funnel, the *Lady Moyra* carried the coat of arms of the Furness Railway in the centre of her paddle box. The bridge and after deckhouse windows were similarly etched. In 1933 her paddle box emblem was replaced by the Brighton coat of arms, as shown here. At the same time the bridge and after deckhouse windows were replaced, etched with the P. & A. Campbell houseflag. (Edwin Keen)

A grandstand view of the outbound White Star liner *Olympic* for the *Brighton Queen's* passengers, off the Isle of Wight in 1933. (Stephen Phillips collection)

Opposite above: With the *Britannia* ahead of her and the *Brighton Queen* on her port side, the Cunard liner *Queen Mary* steams down Southampton Water on her maiden voyage to New York on Wednesday 27 May 1936. The *Glen Gower* was also in attendance but, being slower than the other two White Funnel steamers, was trailing behind, out of the photograph. Astern of the *Queen Mary*, slightly on her port quarter, is the Red Funnel paddle steamer *Lorna Doone*.

Left: Aboard *Brighton Queen* on the round trip from Brighton to Bristol, 24 September 1935.

Below: A less-than-glamorous photograph of the *Brighton Queen*, taken prior to her external painting in the early spring of 1934. (H.G. Owen)

Brighton Queen laid up at Newhaven on Thursday 10 June 1937. The Coronation of King George VI took place on Wednesday 12 May 1937 and was followed by a Review of the Fleet in Spithead during the following week. P. & A. Campbell Ltd, as usual, made the most of such an opportunity for good business by ensuring that the White Funnel Fleet would be well represented at the occasion. The *Britannia, Cambria, Glen Usk* and *Devonia* were sent down for the event, as well as the three South Coast steamers of that season – *Waverley, Glen Gower* and *Brighton Queen*. As the last-named did not normally begin running on the Sussex coast until mid-June, she was taken out of service following her Review sailings. The company considered it uneconomical to run her prior to the busy part of the season. Neither was it economical to bring her home to Bristol, only to send her south again after a short period. She was, therefore, laid up at Newhaven between Saturday 22 May, when her crew were temporarily paid off, and Saturday 19 June, when she re-entered service.

With Capt. W.A. (Bill) Couves blowing the customary three blasts of farewell on the whistle, the *Brighton Queen* leaves Palace Pier, Brighton, for Bristol on the morning of Monday 19 September 1938. (H.A. Allen)

This return trip began at 10.30 a.m. in sunny weather with a fresh wind. However, conditions deteriorated during the course of the day and by the time she passed Portland at 6 p.m. the wind was steadily increasing in force. The log book states:

11.06 p.m. Eddystone abeam. Wind WSW backing to southerly gale. Heavy sea. Rain squalls. Vessel shipping water and labouring heavily.

However, she arrived safely at Hotwells Landing Stage, Bristol, at 4.38 p.m. the following day, after calling at Ilfracombe and Cardiff. A final note in the log states:

Between the hours of 10 p.m. on the 19th and 2.45 a.m. on the 20th, in a southerly gale and heavy seas, the two port wings were badly damaged and rails on the port side forward were set back.

The *Brighton Queen* was destined to spend one more season on the South Coast before being recalled to Bristol earlier than scheduled (with the *Waverley* and *Glen Gower*) on Saturday 2 September 1939, the day before war was declared. The *Brighton Queen*, once again having been requisitioned by the Admiralty for minesweeping duties, met her tragic end during the evacuation of Dunkirk. She left Dunkirk harbour, having already completed one successful round trip, just before noon on 1 June 1940, with about 700 mainly Moroccan soldiers aboard. Twenty minutes later, off the Dyke Shoal, she was attacked by enemy aircraft and was struck by a 500lb bomb aft of the starboard paddle box. She sank within seven minutes with the loss of half of her complement.

In Barry Railway ownership, the *Devonia* arrives at Ilfracombe, 1907/1909.

The Barry Railway Company ceased running steamers at the end of the 1909 season. The *Devonia* (and her consorts *Barry* and *Westonia*) were then purchased by a new company known as Bristol Channel Passenger Boats Ltd, for whom they ran during 1910 and 1911. Whereas in their Barry Railway days the ships were kept in pristine condition, under their new owners standards were not so high, and they began to look very unkempt. This is all too obvious from the saloon strake in the above photograph, showing passengers aboard the *Devonia* about to leave Ilfracombe for Clovelly on 26 August 1911.

Devonia at the Mardyke Wharf, Bristol, in the winter of 1913/1914.

At the end of 1911, Bristol Channel Passenger Boats Ltd ceased trading and their three steamers eventually passed into Campbell's hands. The 1914 season was cut short by the declaration of war on 4 August and the *Devonia* was one of the first steamers to be withdrawn from service.

At the start of the war, a major problem facing the Royal Navy was large-scale German minelaying and a grave shortage of minesweepers. The White Funnel steamers laid up at Bristol came under the scrutiny of a local naval lieutenant, Arthur L. Sanders. He was familiar with the steamers and was well aware of their speed, manoeuvrability and shallow draught. It is not certain whether or not Lieutenant Sanders was solely responsible for suggesting that they would make ideal minesweepers, but there is little doubt that he was one of the prime movers behind their initial trials. Of the steamers available, it appeared that the *Brighton Queen* and *Devonia* would be the most suitable. Accordingly, they were taken in hand by the shipyard workers for conversion. On their trials they proved eminently suitable for the task, and their commissioning into the Royal Navy pioneered the requisition of many more of the country's paddle steamers.

Opposite above: HMS *Devonia* in the Cumberland Basin on Saturday 3 May 1919, the day after she returned to Bristol following her war service.

Opposite below: The *Devonia* arriving at Ilfracombe in 1920. She was decommissioned by the Admiralty on 9 June 1919. An extensive refit then followed, including a three-month spell in Stothert's Dry Dock from March to June 1920, before she re-entered civilian service on Monday 5 July 1920. Further extensive work took place during the winter of 1920/1921, which included the fitting of completely new funnels.

Above and below: The *Devonia* leaving Cardiff (above) in 1920 and (below) in 1922.

With her sponson doors closed and the swell lifting her starboard paddle out of the water, the *Devonia* arrives at Ilfracombe in 1922.

In 1923 P. & A. Campbell Ltd resumed their pre-war association with the Sussex coast resorts with the *Devonia*, *Ravenswood* and *Brighton Belle*. The *Devonia* performed most of the longer coastal trips and the continental sailings but on this particular day she was engaged on shorter journeys. The photograph was taken by W. A. Pelly, the company's Eastbourne agent and accomplished amateur photographer. On the back Mr Pelly has pencilled the details: '*Devonia* returning to Eastbourne pier from a cruise to Seaford Bay, 4.50 p.m., June 20 1923.'

Devonia arriving at Ventnor pier in the 1920s.

Aboard the *Devonia* during a crossing from Hastings to Boulogne in the 1920s.

Devonia at sea, 1923/1924.

Since their purchase by P. & A. Campbell Ltd, something of a problem had been experienced with both the *Devonia* and *Lady Moyra*. It had been found that when they were travelling at speed the bow wave which they generated choked their paddle boxes. This caused excessive vibration and also put a strain on the paddles and engines. Peter and Alec were determined to solve the problem and, in 1926, engaged a photographer to take a series of photographs from his boat of the *Devonia* approaching the Brighton piers. I understand that a large number of such photographs were taken but the one reproduced here is the only one to have survived and probably demonstrates the problem most clearly.

During their dry docking the following winter, bow wave deflector plates were fitted to both vessels. These were rectangular steel plates, fixed to their hulls just on the waterline, in line with the forward end of the sponsons, and which projected outwards at an angle equal to that of the line of the sponsons. The problem was solved. Although the bow wave still rose to the level of the sponsons the deflector plates pushed it out of the way of the paddles.

Incidentally, one reason why some of the die-hard Campbell employees disliked the former Barry Railway steamers was because of the concentric slat openings of their paddle boxes which, they said, would always be more prone to choking than the 'Campbell fashion' fan openings.

With the French tricolour flying from her foremast, the *Devonia* enters Boulogne harbour during the 1920s. The cross-channel excursions usually allowed about four hours ashore, which gave the passengers plenty of time to enjoy the delights of the old town – a climb up the Grand Rue to visit the Cathedral of Notre Dame within the town walls; a leisurely stroll along the picturesque quayside and promenade and, perhaps, a visit to the casino, the top of which is visible behind the bow of the *Devonia*. (Lionel Vaughan collection)

Devonia at Boulogne, about 1930.

Right: On board the *Devonia* on one of her round trips from Brighton to Bristol.

Below: A far cry from the summer sunshine and decks thronged with passengers! On a bitterly cold and foggy January morning in 1933, the *Devonia* lies in Bristol's Floating Harbour. The bridge brasswork has been covered; the reserve deck and bridge windows have been boarded up, and steel covers have been placed on top of the funnel cowls to prevent rain entering and birds nesting in them. Down below it was a different story – her machinery was being overhauled and much painting and varnishing was in progress. Her external redecoration was to begin in the spring, to ready her to take over the Swansea station from the *Lady Moyra*. (H.G. Owen)

Devonia arriving at Swansea in 1933. (H.G. Owen)

Devonia arriving at Ilfracombe in August 1933. (H.G. Owen)

Above: Prior to the 1934 season most of the White Funnel steamers were fitted with chime whistles. The exceptions were the *Britannia,* which was fitted with one from new; the *Brighton Queen,* which had been so equipped during the previous year; and the *Cambria,* which never had one. The chime whistles replaced the organ variety and gave a much more harmonious sound. (The notes B flat, D and G, played in unison on a keyboard will give an idea.) In this photograph of the *Devonia,* taken at Bristol on 9 June 1934, the modification is being carried out. (Edwin Keen)

Right: Devonia at the Mardyke Wharf, Bristol, in the spring of 1936. (H.G. Owen)

Devonia at anchor off Lundy in company with the Bideford–Lundy packet *Lerina*, 1936/1937.

Above: Devonia arriving at Swansea, after her morning trip to Ilfracombe on a Saturday in 1935. (H.G. Owen)

Left: Devonia resting on the mud at Pockett's Wharf, Swansea, at low water on a spring tide in the 1930s. (H.G. Owen)

The magnificent paddle box of the *Devonia*. At its centre is the coat of arms of Exeter – the county town of Devon. This replaced the Barry Railway's emblem during the course of her post-war refit in 1920. (Edwin Keen)

Following the Coronation of King George VI a Review of the Fleet was held at Spithead on Thursday 20 May 1937. The White Funnel Fleet was well represented at the event by seven of its steamers – *Britannia*, *Cambria*, *Glen Usk* and *Devonia* – which were sent around from the Bristol Channel, as well as the three South Coast steamers, *Brighton Queen*, *Waverley* and *Glen Gower*. Here, the *Devonia* is seen at the mouth of the River Avon on her return from the South Coast on the evening of Saturday 22 May 1937. (Edwin Keen)

Devonia leaving Padstow for a cruise in the River Camel in 1938. (Sydney Robinson)

Devonia at Bristol during the spring of 1939; a view which clearly shows the twin lifeboats which had been fitted prior to the 1938 season.

Her high coal consumption had led to her seasons becoming shorter as time passed. In fact, during the late 1930s she was in service for only about six weeks of the year and in 1939, although fully prepared for sailing, she was taken out of service completely for economic reasons.

Shortly after the outbreak of the Second World War she was, for the second time in her career, requisitioned by the Admiralty for minesweeping. During the evacuation of Dunkirk, she was beached and abandoned at La Panne after a salvo of enemy bombs fell close to her stern and rendered her unseaworthy. Rumours that she was later salvaged and put into service on one of the German rivers have never been substantiated.

two

The River Avon and an
Accident Black Spot

Of all the rivers which flow into the Bristol Channel, and which were navigated by the
excursion steamers, the most hazardous and potentially dangerous was the River Avon.
The broad sweep of its course past Avonmouth, then upstream past the village of Pill, gives
way to a narrower and more tortuous passage from Hungroad, through the spectacular
Avon Gorge to Hotwells landing stage and the entrance to the Floating Harbour; the
bends, mud banks and tidal flows conspire to make its passage a potential nightmare.
Variable speed limits were imposed, which were necessary not only to overcome those
natural hazards, but also to avoid collisions between the large number of ships of varying
sizes entering and leaving the port. The Port of Bristol Authority built signal stations at
Shirehampton and Sea Mills where, over the high water periods, lookouts were posted
to relay information on the shipping movements in the river to each vessel that passed,
originally by megaphone and later by microphone and loudspeakers.

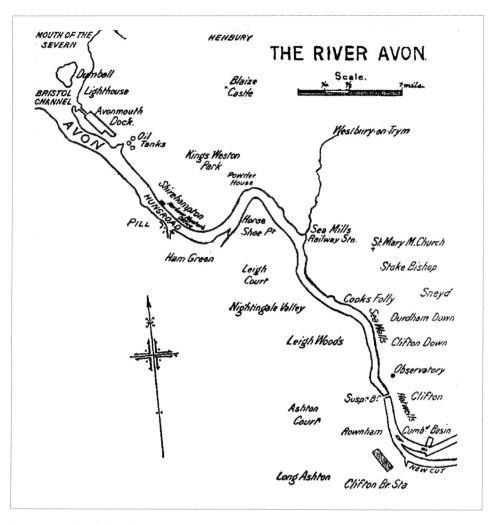

A map reproduced from the *Bristol Channel & District Guide* of 1896 which shows the course of the river used by the excursion steamers.

Opposite above: Glen Usk swinging on a flood tide at Tongue Head – the entrance to the Cumberland Basin locks – on Saturday 14 May 1927. She was on a return cruise from Cardiff, Clevedon and Bristol, up the River Severn.

Opposite below: The Avon Gorge and the Clifton Suspension Bridge in the late 1890s. The *Westward Ho* lies at Hotwells Landing Stage.

Above: A view of Hotwells from the Clifton Suspension Bridge in the 1900s, with the *Cambria* at the landing stage.

Opposite above: Devonia making her way from the Cumberland Basin to Hotwells Landing Stage on Friday 2 June 1922. The memorandum book records – '12 noon. *Devonia* out on a level…' – an expression frequently used to denote that the water level in the basin was the same as that in the river, thus saving time by avoiding the necessity to 'lock out'. (Edwin Keen)

The problems of navigating in the narrow confines of the River Avon were highlighted in a newspaper report of July 1923:

A COLLISION IN THE AVON

In the Admiralty Court, the owners of the steamship *City of Amiens* brought an action against the owners of the steamer *Devonia* of Bristol, claiming damages for a collision in the River Avon on the evening of 9 September 1922.

After the hearing Mr Justice Hill, delivering his judgement, stated that he found the *Devonia* alone to blame for the collision which occurred just above the Clifton Suspension Bridge. The *City of Amiens* was leaving for Barry and the *Devonia* was arriving with passengers from Cardiff.

His Lordship said he could not find that the *City of Amiens*, in leaving with the tide, sheered into the paddle steamer, as the defendants had said, encroaching on defendant's water. The beam of the two vessels was such that in this narrow channel either might get something over the middle line but the *City of Amiens* passed successively and safely vessels as she came out, and was clearly well under control. On the other hand the *Devonia*, with which he sympathised, had to steady for a signal against her and other craft, and it looked as though when the way was taken off, the set of the tide at this point carried her over. There was a time when she ported her helm, and it might be said that in getting a swing, her bows escaped the *City of Amiens*, which she then struck with her port sponson. He was satisfied that if the *Devonia* had seen her sooner she might have kept clear. The *Devonia* was alone to blame.

At the directors' meeting on 20 November 1923 the secretary reported that a cheque for £512 10s had been sent in settlement of the claim by the owners of the *City of Amiens* for damage sustained in the collision.

On a remarkably still and hazy morning, with the river as smooth as glass, the *Brighton Belle* passes Leigh Woods on a day trip to Barry, Whit Sunday 15 May 1932. (Edwin Keen)

River Avon, & Portway, Bristol.

Britannia making her way upriver in the early 1930s. She has just passed, on her port side, the rocky promontory known as Sea Walls, and is approaching Leigh Woods to starboard.

Undoubtedly the River Avon's most hazardous obstacle was the Horseshoe Bend. What makes the rounding of this bend particularly precarious is the flow of the tide. On fast-flowing spring tides, a safe passage can be accomplished only within an hour and a half either side of high water. Before or after that period, apart from the obvious problem of insufficient water, the river flows at such a rate that a ship, inbound on the flood or outbound on the ebb, would run a grave risk of being swept onto the mud on the river's Gloucestershire bank. On the slower neap tides the timing is a little less critical, but the hazards remain.

During the era of the excursion steamers the bend claimed a number of victims, ranging from little more than 'touches' on the mud to more serious groundings, the worst of which was the potentially fatal predicament of the *Glen Usk* in 1959. Nevertheless, considering the number of journeys made up and down the river by the excursions steamers over the years, accidents were relatively few.

Opposite above and below: Meeting another vessel on the bend called for great caution. These two successive photographs, taken in the early 1900s, show the *Cambria* and a cargo vessel approaching each other at dead slow speed. The two ships having safely passed, the *Cambria* increases speed to give greater steerage way.

Britannia rounding the Horseshoe Bend in the 1900s. At that time she was under the command of Capt. Peter Campbell who, not for the first time, appears to be breaking the speed limit. Capt. Peter was not alone in this breach of regulations; the newspapers occasionally carried reports such as the following, which appeared in the *Western Mail* on 10 July 1894:

CAPTAINS CONVICTED FOR TOO RAPID STEAMING

The Bristol magistrates, on Monday last, fined Capt. Alexander Campbell of the *Westward Ho*, Capt. Peter Campbell of the *Ravenswood* and Capt. Hucker of the *Lorna Doone* £2 each for proceeding in a part of the River Avon at a higher rate of speed than the bye-laws permit – they exceeded the 9 knot limit, running as fast as 15 knots in one case.

The photograph is interesting as it illustrates another reason for the speed limits – the excessive wash which caused severe erosion of the riverbanks.

Ravenswood in the 1930s.

On the afternoon of Sunday 27 July 1947, the *Cardiff Queen,* on a cruise to the English & Welsh Grounds Lightvessel, temporarily ran aground. Fortunately, the tide was on the flood and she soon refloated, undamaged. (Grahame Farr)

Bristol Queen, 1952.

Above and below: Glen Gower, 1955. (Ernest Dumbleton)

Bristol Queen, 1955.

Further downriver, the *Glen Usk* passes the old Custom House at Pill, 8 September 1946. (Edwin Keen)

Opposite above: Glen Usk aground on Saturday 30 August 1959, having left Hotwells a little too late on the ebb tide. Her passengers disembarked by way of two gangways from the starboard sponson and, with the help of the police and fire brigade, had to negotiate 100 yards of muddy river bank, a 50ft steel ladder, a railway line and a further rough track to the Portway, where alternative transport was waiting to return them to their points of departure. Later that night the *Glen Usk* was left high and dry over the low water period. Despite heeling over to an alarming angle, the subsequent dry dock inspection found that she was little the worse for the experience. Full details of the incident can be found in *White Funnels – The story of P. & A. Campbell Steamers 1946-1968.*

Opposite below: Westward Ho passing Pill in the 1920s. The Shirehampton signal station can be seen on the Gloucestershire bank on her port side.

Having negotiated the river, the *Glen Gower* approaches full speed as she passes Avonmouth and heads into the Severn Estuary in 1932.

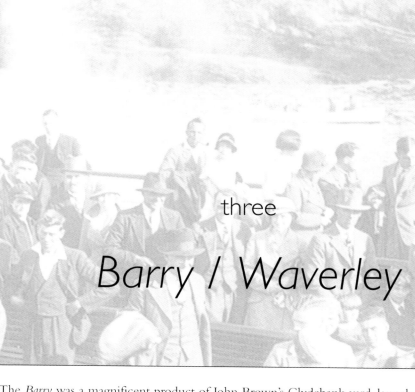

three

Barry / Waverley

The *Barry* was a magnificent product of John Brown's Clydebank yard, launched for the Barry Railway Company on 4 May 1907. She became a consort of the 'Beautiful Sisters', *Gwalia* and *Devonia*, and caught the eye of Capt. Peter Campbell, who declared her to be one of the 'prettiest' paddle steamers he had ever seen and one which he would like to own. Along with the *Devonia* and *Westonia*, the *Barry* passed into the ownership of Bristol Channel Passenger Boats in 1910. That company ceased trading after two years and in 1912 she passed into Campbell hands. Capt. Peter's wish had come true. She was a most useful vessel, economical on fuel, a good, if lively, sea boat and with a good passenger-carrying capacity. Not surprisingly, she became a 'maid of all work'.

Barry arriving at Ilfracombe, 1908/1909.

Barry in the Avon, 1911.

Barry off Ilfracombe in 1912.

Barry leaving Cardiff in the early 1920s. She had been requisitioned by the Admiralty during the First World War and travelled far afield. The full details of her exploits in the Eastern Mediterranean are fully documented in my book *A Dangerous Occupation*. On her return to civilian service, her first duty was to begin the White Funnel Fleet's regular sailings from Swansea on 22 May 1920.

Damage to the *Barry* sustained in September 1921.

A significant feature of the *Barry's* White Funnel career was that it was relatively uneventful. However, during 1921, the continuing rivalry between P. & A. Campbell Ltd and Tucker's Yellow Funnel Fleet was the cause of an unfortunate accident on the evening of Saturday 17 September. The memorandum book gives the details:

> *Barry* was off Weston at 9.05 p.m. and made for the pier when *Lady Evelyn*, also making for the pier, came straight across *Barry's* port bow. *Barry* had to come ahead or go on to the rocks (strong easterly wind and ebb tide) and in coming out under the *Lady Evelyn's* stern had her galley badly stove in along with the fore part of the starboard paddle box.

Considerable repairs were necessary, which led to the *Barry's* withdrawal from service and her return to Bristol the following day.

This photograph is also of interest with regard to the vessel's paddle box emblem – the arms of the Barry Railway Company. The dragon was painted red and its surrounding frame carried the legend 'Barry Railway Company 1884' in gold, surmounted by a stag's head. This was the form in which it appeared on the steamer as built. On her acquisition by P. & A. Campbell Ltd, the lettering was removed and the dragon, like the original colour of the stag's head, became gold-leafed. An interesting story concerning this device is recounted on page 64.

Opposite above: Barry arriving at Ilfracombe in the early 1920s.

Opposite below: Waverley leaving Hotwells landing stage in 1925. Prior to that season the *Barry* was renamed, thus perpetuating the name of the first White Funnel steamer to sail in the Bristol Channel.

Above: In 1926 it was decided to send the *Waverley* to the South Coast in place of the *Ravenswood*. The reasons were two-fold. Passenger figures were on the increase and the *Waverley's* larger capacity was required, and the Board of Trade would no longer allow open foredeck vessels, such as the *Ravenswood*, to cross the Channel. Although the *Devonia* maintained the continental excursions, the company found it desirable to have a second vessel to supplement her on that service during the height of the season. The *Waverley* is seen here in Hill's Dry Dock, Bristol in March 1926 having a bow rudder fitted – an asset when turning the ship in the harbours at Newhaven and Boulogne. (H.G. Owen)

The *Waverley* arriving at Eastbourne in 1926.

The early part of her first season on the south coast was marred by an accident, strikes and consequent coal shortages. She arrived at Newhaven on Tuesday 30 March, ran her first trips two days later on Maundy Thursday and made her first trip to Boulogne on Easter Sunday 4 April. On Wednesday 14 April she damaged her rudder while turning in Newhaven harbour and had to be taken onto the gridiron for repairs, which necessitated the cancellation of three days' sailings. The miners' strike began on Saturday 1 May, followed by the General Strike the following Monday. On that day the *Waverley* was at anchor off Brighton, precariously short of coal and with little chance of replenishing her bunkers in the foreseeable future. All of her personnel, apart from a skeleton crew, were given forty-eight hours' notice and on the morning of Thursday 6 May she disembarked them at Palace Pier, from where they returned to Bristol by charabanc. The *Waverley* then proceeded to Newhaven to be laid up. A sufficient supply of coal was released to enable her to resume her sailings from Saturday 22 May, and from then on she coaled at Boulogne whenever possible. This was a procedure followed by all of the cross-Channel White Funnel steamers, not only in 1926 but throughout their long connection with the Sussex coast. The reason was simple – the best quality Scottish steam coal, which the company favoured, was cheaper in France than in the UK!

Opposite below: The *Waverley* in dry dock in company with the *Brighton Belle* in March 1926. Such a procedure was followed, as far as possible, in order to save on docking dues. (H.G. Owen)

A view from the foredeck of the *Waverley* off the Sussex coast in the mid–1920s. On the bridge is Capt. Frank Weeks, a most popular and respected master who enjoyed a long association with P. & A. Campbell's South Coast services. He was, incidentally, the father of the late BBC sports commentator Alan Weeks.

Above and below: Shortly before leaving the Bristol Channel for the South Coast, the *Waverley* arrives and departs from Bristol on an afternoon cruise up the River Severn, Sunday 18 June 1933. (E.R. Keen)

Waverley arriving at Eastbourne pier on 23 August 1933.

Waverley arriving at Ilfracombe in 1934. (H.G. Owen)

The *Waverley* ran on the South Coast from 1926 until the end of the 1933 season. From 1934 she no longer satisfied the Board of Trade's changing structural requirements for cross-Channel vessels. She was therefore replaced by the *Glen Gower*, which had been suitably modified by the addition of an extra bulkhead. The *Waverley* returned to Bristol Channel duties during 1934 and 1935 – rather fortuitously, as she replaced the *Cambria* and *Britannia* while they underwent major refits which caused them to miss entire seasons, the *Britannia* in 1934 and *Cambria* in 1935. She proved a worthy substitute for those two vessels, coping admirably with their arduous, down-Channel schedules.

verley at Ilfracombe pier in 1934. (H.G. Owen)

sengers aboard the *Waverley* at Ilfracombe, 1934/1935.

On a wet and blustery day in 1936, the *Waverley* arrives at the West Pier, Brighton.

During the summer of 1935, despite predominantly indifferent weather, the three South Coast steamers, *Brighton Queen, Glen Gower* and *Brighton Belle*, had been sorely tried in coping with the passenger traffic. The company decided, therefore, to experiment with four steamers in 1936. Now that the *Britannia* and *Cambria* were once again fully operational in the Bristol Channel, the Waverley returned to the South Coast. Unfortunately, the weather during that season was very poor, with much wind and rain, leading to poor passenger figures and many curtailed and cancelled trips. The experiment was not repeated although, from 1937 to 1939, the *Waverley* replaced the smaller *Brighton Belle* on the Sussex coast.

STORMBOUND AT NEWHAVEN (following four photgraphs)

Brighton Queen. (H.A. Allen)

Glen Gower. (H.A. Allen)

Opposite below: The four South Coast steamers, *Brighton Queen, Glen Gower, Brighton Belle* and *Waverley,* stormbound in Newhaven harbour on Tuesday 8 September 1936. (H.A. Allen)

Brighton Belle and *Waverley*. (H.A. Allen)

The story referred to on page 54, concerning the *Waverley*'s paddle box emblem, has its origins in the wet and windy summer of 1936. It has often been stated that the stags' heads were removed during the late 1930s on the whim of an employee of the company. This is not the whole story. The facts are that towards the end of the 1936 season, the stag's head on one paddle box (I have been unable to ascertain whether port or starboard) worked loose, and before it could be repaired it disappeared altogether. The loss was discovered one evening in Newhaven harbour after the *Waverley* had spent most of the day rolling along the coast in a heavy English Channel swell. It was therefore concluded that the sea was responsible for washing it off. During her following winter overhaul the question of the missing stag's head was considered. It was felt that the cost of having a gold-leafed replacement carved would be prohibitive, so it was decided to remove the one which remained and to modify both paddle boxes. No close-up photographs exist showing the alterations, but the photograph on page 66 shows the detail reasonably clearly.

Waverley at Bournemouth Pier in 1937.

Above and below: Waverley arriving at Newhaven in 1937.

Above and below: Waverley steaming down-Channel past Battery Point, Portishead, on Saturday 28 May 1938. The following Monday she left Cardiff at 7.15 a.m. bound for the South Coast. High winds and heavy seas hindered her progress down-Channel and her departure from Ilfracombe was delayed for five hours in the hope of the weather moderating. The wind had eased sufficiently for her to proceed at 3.43 p.m. but she battled against a very heavy swell on the journey down the Cornish coast. The memorandum book entry for Tuesday 31 May records '*Waverley* arrived Newhaven 5.20 p.m. Heavy swell. All well'.

This idyllic sunset view is somewhat overshadowed by the rapidly developing tension in Europe. Just over a year later the country was at war with Germany, and the *Waverley* was once again in Admiralty hands, sweeping mines off the Northumberland coast. During one such operation, on 5 July 1941, she was attacked and sunk by enemy aircraft.

four

The Ailsa Quartet

The Ailsa Shipbuilding Co. of Troon had earned a reputation for turning out many fine vessels. It was to this company that P. & A. Campbell Ltd turned in 1910 for an up-to-date, economical steamer for service on the Cardiff to Weston ferry. Speed was not a particularly important feature, but a small engine with low fuel consumption was. This, in turn, would mean small paddle wheels and low paddle boxes allowing five gangways at a time to be used to facilitate fast embarking and disembarking. The steamer began service in the beautiful summer of 1911 and was an instant success. She was named *Lady Ismay,* after Lady Ismay Crichton Stuart, the daughter of the Marquis of Bute – Cardiff's most prominent citizen. The Campbell brothers were so impressed with their new acquisition that two similar vessels were subsequently ordered – *Glen Avon,* which began service in 1912, followed by *Glen Usk* in 1914.

The depletion of the White Funnel Fleet during the First World War led Peter and Alec to the Troon company again in 1919, seeking a larger version of the *Glen Usk:* the *Glen Gower* of 1922.

Lady Ismay
in Hill's Dry
Dock, Bristol,
in the spring
of 1912.

Lady Ismay at Hotwells landing stage in 1912.

dy Ismay off Ilfracombe in fresh weather, 1912.

dy Ismay arriving at Cardiff in 1913.

he *Lady Ismay* was destined to lead a short life. She came to a tragic end on 21 December 1915
hen she struck a mine near the Longsand Lightvessel, off Harwich, while engaged in minesweeping
erations. She sank in less than a minute with considerable loss of life.

Glen Avon leaving Newport on her maiden trip – an afternoon cruise to Bristol – on Saturday 14 July 1912. (Lionel Vaughan collection)

Glen Avon in the River Avon on her maiden trip.

Glen Avon outward-bound from Bristol in 1914.

The *Glen Avon* served with distinction as a minesweeper in the First World War and came through the hostilities with barely a scratch. However, her Admiralty service came to a sudden end after the Armistice when she collided with the cargo steamer *J.E. O'Neill*, on 10 February 1919, while engaged in mine-clearance duties in the Thames estuary. She was towed to Bristol and was then towed to Troon by the Admiralty tug *Roll Call* for refitting by her builders. She is seen here leaving Troon at 8 p.m. on Saturday 5 July 1919, to return to the Bristol Channel. Her journey south was uneventful – she passed the South Bishop Lighthouse (off the Pembrokeshire coast) at 11.45 a.m. on Sunday 6 July 1919; the Scarweather Lightvessel (in Swansea Bay) at 5.12 p.m., and arrived in Bristol at 12.30 a.m. the following day.

Above: Glen Avon leaving Cardiff in 1920.

Left: During the early part of the First World War, Penarth Pier had been requisitioned by the Royal Engineers. At the end of the conflict, owing to the lack of maintenance, considerable renovations and repairs were necessary, which were not completed until February 1926. The first steamer to call was the *Glen Avon,* seen here arriving at the pier for the opening ceremony on Wednesday 7 April 1926.

Opposite below: Glen Avon approaching Hotwells landing stage in 1933. (H.G. Owen)

ove: Glen Avon arriving at Weston, 1929. (H.G. Owen)

iring the inter-war period the *Glen Avon* was the mainstay of P. & A. Campbell's Cardiff to Weston
ry, and she was usually the first steamer out and the last in. This service was the company's 'bread and
ter' - well-patronised day trips down-Channel by the larger steamers certainly generated acceptable
ings, but fuel and catering costs ate into the profits. The *Glen Avon*, however, with her interminable
s between Cardiff and Weston, sometimes carrying thousands of passengers in a day at the height of
season, really brought in the money!

The *Glen Avon* steaming down the Avon Gorge on Saturday 12 May 1934. (Edwin Keen)

Opposite page: Although she spent most of her career on the ferry route, the *Glen Avon* did occasionally venture down-Channel. Her consorts sometimes supplemented her during the busiest times of the season, and now and then replaced her, allowing her to journey farther afield. She is pictured above arriving at Ilfracombe, and below, at anchor off Clovelly, 1934/1935. (H.G. Owen)

Glen Avon arriving at Bristol, from Cardiff, on Wednesday 3 July 1935. Wednesday was early closing day in Cardiff and the regular afternoon trip up the River Avon proved to be a great attraction. (Edwin Keen)

Glen Avon at the Underfall Yard, Bristol, on Sunday 6 October 1935. She had just finished her season, which had begun on Wednesday 17 April. She was requisitioned by the Admiralty in 1939, initially for minesweeping duties and later as an anti-aircraft ship. In August 1944, she was detailed to act as an examination vessel and guard ship off the Normandy coast, following the D-Day landings. It was on this station that she sank in a severe storm, near Arromanches, on 2 September 1944. (Edwin Keen)

Above and below: Glen Usk on trials in the Firth of Clyde on 27 May 1914.

Glen Usk leaving Newport in 1914.

Glen Usk off Portishead, 1914.

The newly built *Glen Usk* ran her maiden trip on Whit Monday 1 June 1914, and had been in service for just over two months before being laid up at Bristol following the outbreak of the First World War. She was requisitioned by the Admiralty for minesweeping duties and within a year of entering service was back at Troon where, in company with the *Britannia,* she formed part of the flotilla known as the 'Clyde Paddlers'. After sweeping in the Firth of Clyde the flotilla was transferred to Northern Ireland and later to the Firth of Forth, where the *Glen Usk* gained the distinction of being present at the surrender of the German High Seas Fleet on 21 November 1918.

Above and below: Glen Usk leaving Swansea in 1920. Her post-war refit took place at the Harland & Wolff yard in Govan, Glasgow, after which she re-entered civilian service on Saturday 6 September 1919 for a 'season' of only four weeks. Her first full season began the following year.

Glen Usk in the River Avon in the 1920s. (H.G. Owen)

Glen Usk arriving at Weston in 1929. (H.G. Owen)

Glen Usk in the Floating Harbour, Bristol, on Sunday 9 April 1933. Her winter overhaul is nearing completion, in preparation for the start of the season the following week. (H.G. Owen)

Glen Usk leaving Swansea in 1934. (H.G. Owen)

Glen Usk at Ilfracombe, 1938/1939.

The *Glen Usk*'s Second World War service, during which she served as a minesweeper, anti-aircraft ship and supply ship, ended in Holland after a spell as a floating hostel for the New Waterway pilots. She returned to Bristol in October 1946 and her refit was rapidly completed, following the withdrawal of the *Britannia* after her boiler failure.

This photograph shows the *Glen Usk* at a somewhat unusual angle at Ilfracombe in 1948. During the few hours in which she had lain at the Stone Bench, a southerly gale had blown up. To manoeuvre her into the channel for her return trip, her master, Capt. Findlay Brander, displayed his consummate ship-handling skills by backing her away from the pier and simply letting the wind blow her broadside out of the harbour. He then brought her in a semicircle close to the pier, at which point the photograph was taken, from where she swept out to sea. (H.G. Owen)

en Usk leaving Cardiff in 1949.

en Usk at Minehead on an evening cruise from Cardiff in 1951. Trips to the Somerset resort had
umed on 2 June that year after the harbour had been dredged sufficiently to allow the steamers to call,
pier having been demolished on military orders during the Second World War. (H.G. Owen)

Glen Usk, full to capacity with passengers from Cardiff and Penarth, arriving at Weston on the morning of Easter Monday, 19 April 1954. (Edwin Keen)

During the First World War, two of the White Funnel steamers, the *Brighton Queen* and the *Lady Ismay*, were lost as a result of enemy action. After the hostilities it was found that a further three, the *Waverley, Glen Rosa* and *Albion*, were found to be beyond economic repair and were broken up. The company, therefore, was in need of additional tonnage. In 1919 a steamer was ordered from the Ailsa Shipbuilding Co. of Troon but the delivery of 'No. 377' was delayed by a combination of shipyard strikes and shortages of materials.

The Ailsa Shipbuilding Company's yard on 23 August 1921. On the left, the steamer *Jose Menendez* is about to be launched, and on the right, No. 377 is on the stocks, plated up, with decks laid but no deckhouses. She was eventually launched on 14 February 1922 and appropriately named *Glen Gower*, as she was to be stationed at Swansea.

Opposite below: Glen Usk leaving Bristol on Sunday 30 August 1959. (Norman Bird)

Later that evening, following her late departure for Cardiff on a falling tide, she ran on to the mud of the Gloucestershire bank of the River Avon's notorious Horseshoe Bend. (See page 48.) Her passengers were safely disembarked but the vessel heeled over to an alarming angle during the course of the overnight low tide. She was back in service, however, on Wednesday 2 September, after an inspection revealed that the staunch old ship was none the worse for the experience. At the end of her 1960 season she was withdrawn from service and after a period laid up in Penarth dock and later in the East dock, Cardiff, ended her days at the breaker's yard at Passage West, Cork, in the spring of 1963.

Glen Gower at the fitting-out berth in May 1922. She is almost ready to put to sea – the Mumbles Head carvings are in place on the paddle boxes, the canvas covers are on the lifeboats, the jib and trysail have been fitted and steam is being raised for her trials.

Glen Gower returning to Troon harbour following her satisfactory trials in the Firth of Clyde on Wednesday 24 May 1922. Her funnels are scorched from the intense heat generated by pushing her to her limit. Her average trial speed of 17.25 knots was 0.25 knots faster than that guaranteed by her builders. Her second-hand engines, removed from the White Funnel steamer *Albion* when she had been broken up at Troon after the war, dated from 1893 and proved to be as good as new.

Aboard the *Glen Gower*, under the command of Capt. Duncan Smith, on her delivery voyage from Troon to Bristol on 25/26 May 1922. On the left is company director Mr W.H. Brown and on the right, Capt. Daniel Taylor.

Mr Brown again, in the centre of the back row with Capt. Taylor on his right. I have been unable to identify the others.

Grattan Phillipse's photograph of the *Glen Gower* arriving at Ilfracombe on her maiden trip, from Bristol, on Friday 2 June 1922. On the back of the photograph George Owen noted:

Left Hotwells pontoon 12.30 p.m., arrived Ilfracombe, (direct run), 4.27 p.m. – 3 hours 57 minutes in strong head wind and choppy sea, 68 passengers. At the telegraphs Capt. Duncan Smith; at the wheel, mate Fred Nunn. Peter Campbell on the bridge wearing bowler hat; man wearing cap and light raincoat is Gordon Fry, Capt. Peter's son in law. On the paddle box, Billy Browning, from St. Ives – bosun. Ship sailed light to Swansea that evening at 7.15 in readiness to begin her season on the following morning – Whit Saturday – with 9.15 a.m. sailing to Ilfracombe.

Glen Gower arriving at Ilfracombe on her first sailing from Swansea and Mumbles on Whit Saturday, 3 June 1922.

Glen Gower leaving Porthcawl on a cruise after an early morning trip from Swansea to Ilfracombe on Whit Monday, 5 June 1922.

Glen Gower leaving Ilfracombe for Clovelly, 1922.

Glen Gower lying astern of the training ship HMS *Flying Fox* at the Mardyke Wharf, Bristol, Sunday 21 April 1929. (H.G. Owen)

Opposite above: Britannia, Westward Ho, Devonia, Glen Gower and *Cambria* at Ilfracombe, Saturday 15 July 1922. On every other day of the week, most of the steamers would run trips out of Ilfracombe. Saturdays, however, were the holiday-makers' arrival and departure days, when there was little demand for such trips. The steamers would therefore either anchor offshore or remain at the pier waiting to return to their destinations in the evening. On this occasion, owing to the low tide, the steamers are berthed at the face of the pier. Over the high water period the ships would be berthed inside the pier at the Stone Bench. This position was always preferable as it facilitated quicker and easier embarking and disembarking, by avoiding the necessity for passengers to negotiate flights of stone steps.

Opposite below: Lunch 'al fresco' aboard the *Glen Gower* at Ilfracombe pier in the early 1920s.

Glen Gower arriving at Ilfracombe on Whit Monday, 9 June 1930, with 1,066 passengers aboard. She had taken on 1,077 at Cardiff – two less than the maximum number permitted on her No. 3 certificate (Bristol–Lundy). She had also called at Minehead and off Lynmouth. (H.G. Owen)

Opposite above: Glen Gower arriving at Swansea after a morning trip to Ilfracombe on Saturday 8 July 1933. Saturdays were busy days for the Swansea steamer; at the height of each season there were often three or four return crossings to Ilfracombe, with the ship completing her sailings during the early hours of Sunday morning. (H.G. Owen)

Opposite below: Glen Gower leaving Swansea in July 1947. (H.G. Owen)

The *Glen Gower's* Second World War service, during which she served as a minesweeper and anti-aircraft ship, ended in Antwerp where she was employed as a transport vessel for the RAF personnel at the Scheldt balloon barrage. Following her return to Bristol in June 1945 she underwent an extensive refit, before returning to service in May 1947.

Glen Gower leaving the Cumberland Basin for Newport on Saturday 29 May 1954, in readiness to start her season. (Edwin Keen)

At the end of her 1957 season the *Glen Gower* was laid up in Penarth dock. After two years of neglect, during which she was advertised for sale, she was purchased by Belgian shipbreakers. She is seen here in the Penarth dock basin about to leave for Antwerp in tow of the Hull tug, *Tradesman*, on 7 April 1960.

five

Empress Queen

The order for a new, twin-screw turbine steamer was placed with the Ailsa Shipbuilding Co. of Troon on 10 May 1939. It was the company's intention to place her on the Continental service from the summer of 1940, but the outbreak of war changed all that. After her launch on 29 February 1940, she was fitted out as an anti-aircraft ship and served in that capacity, as HMS *Queen Eagle,* in the Thames Estuary until September 1943. She was then taken in hand by a Tilbury shipyard for alterations to her accommodation, and began service as a troop transport between Stranraer and Larne in January 1944, under her original name.

The arrival of the *Empress Queen*, although very welcome, also posed the company with a problem. Government restrictions had been introduced which prohibited Continental day trips, the service for which she was intended, so what was the company to do with her? Her size precluded her from sailing in the upper reaches of the Bristol Channel, so instead she was placed on the lucrative Swansea to Ilfracombe service. The photograph shows her arriving at Swansea, stern first and using her bow rudder, from Bristol on Friday 27 June 1947. She was about to make her maiden civilian trip – an evening cruise around the Scarweather lightvessel. (H.G. Owen)

Opposite above: Empress Queen at Larne on 2 March 1946.

Opposite below: Her troop transport duties ended in October 1946 and she returned to her builders to be refitted for civilian service. She is seen here, following her refit, on trials in the Firth of Clyde on Monday 16 June 1947.

Her length was just over 269ft and her gross tonnage now measured 1,781 tons. She was fitted with four turbines by Harland & Wolff, with a single, double-ended oil-fired boiler which gave her a service speed of 17.5 knots. She was well appointed, with two passenger decks, two dining saloons, a sun lounge, bar and cocktail bar and she could accommodate up to 1,300 passengers.

Above and below: The following morning she left Swansea for her first visit to Ilfracombe. Once again her bow rudder allowed her to leave the river stern first, and avoid the necessity to swing the ship. (H.G. Owen)

On the afternoon of her first visit, Saturday 28 June 1947, the *Empress Queen* lies at the stone bench at Ilfracombe.

Leaving Ilfracombe on her return sailing to Swansea, Saturday 28 June 1947. Her period at Swansea was not a success. She had sustained a number of bumps and scrapes and it became apparent that, despite her bow rudder, the combination of her size and propulsion meant that she lacked the manoeuvrability of the paddle steamers, so essential in the narrow confines of some of the Bristol Channel ports of call. It was decided, therefore, that she would change places with the *Glen Gower*, then running coastal trips from Brighton. The *Empress Queen* was to spend the rest of the 1947 season and subsequent three seasons on the Sussex coast.

The pier at Shanklin, Isle of Wight, was reopened to steamers after the Second World War, the *Britannia* making the first call on Tuesday 8 June 1948. The *Britannia's* consort on the South Coast was the *Empress Queen*, seen here at Shanklin later that season.

Empress Queen leaving Brighton in September 1948.

Above and below: Empress Queen arriving at Bristol on her return from her South Coast season, Tuesday 14 September 1948. (Edwin Keen)

Empress Queen arriving at Brighton in August 1950. Her three seasons at Brighton had not been a success, partly because berthing at the piers was a slow and often difficult process, where, as in the Bristol Channel, paddle steamer manoeuvrability was sadly missed. She also seemed to be impossible to fill with sufficient passengers. These reasons, coupled with the appalling summer weather of 1950, led to her withdrawal from the Sussex coast. Once again alternative employment had to be found for her in the hope of making her pay.

ring 1951 she was based at Torquay, from where, in addition to running coastal cruises, she ran
ularly to Guernsey with a few visits to Alderney. The average number of passengers to Guernsey was
;, just over a half of her capacity, and the three trips to Alderney averaged a mere 137. The photograph
ws her arriving at St Peter Port, Guernsey, on her first trip of the season and maiden trip to the
nd on Monday 25 June 1951; even on this special occasion there were only 198 passengers aboard.
e coastal trips were disastrous, passenger figures being so poor that they were abandoned altogether
m mid-July. By the end of her season, on 16 September, she had lost forty-two sailing days owing to
ombination of the aborted coastal cruises, repairs, off-service days and bad weather. The equivalent of
weeks lost out of a twelve-week season was the last straw. With cross-Channel trips to France still out
the question, she was laid up at Narrow Quay, Bristol, and offered for sale.

npress Queen being towed from the Cumberland Basin, after engine trials, on Tuesday 15 March 1955.
ie is waiting for the Junction Lock road bridge to open in order to make her way into the Floating
arbour and then into Hill's Dry Dock.
During the three years in which she was laid up, several companies expressed an interest in her, but
) firm offer materialised until February 1955 when the three Kavounides brothers, of Athens, offered
30,000 plus £1,000 for a dockside trial. The offer was accepted despite the fact that the asking price
as then £45,000. The results of the engine trials and dry dock inspection were satisfactory, and the
mpress Queen became the property of the Kavounides Shipping Co. Ltd on 1 April 1955. (Ernest Nurse)

At the Railway Wharf, Bristol, on Saturday 2 April 1955, with the Greek flag flying at her stern and steam being raised for the journey to Athens. She had been renamed *Philippos* in memory of the brothers' late father. (Edwin Keen)

Philippos in tow on the River Avon on Sunday 3 April 1955. She was expected to arrive in Piraeus, the port of Athens, nine days later, but owing to bad weather the journey took nearly three weeks.

Her time in Greece was most successful, with well-patronised cruises to the Greek islands and also to Brindisi and Venice. But it came to an end in 1972 when, while undergoing routine maintenance in Piraeus, she caught fire and it spread at alarming speed throughout the ship. Strenuous efforts to put it out failed, leaving a virtually empty and twisted hulk, totally beyond repair – a tragic end after only thirty-two years of service.

six

Passengers and Personalities

Before the First World War, the seaside photographers were as commonplace as the bathing machines and buckets and spades. Among their most lucrative, and therefore favourite subjects, were the steamer passengers. After photographing them on the decks of the steamer on arrival, the plates were passed to an assistant who would then disappear into the darkroom like a rabbit into a burrow. He would develop the plates and make postcard prints, which would be offered for sale to their subjects before their departure later in the day. Such was the volume of the work on busy days that many of the prints would still be wet when displayed for sale. Furthermore, a reduction of the time spent in their processing, particularly the fixing and washing stages, brought about by tight 'deadlines', meant that the prints were doomed to fade with time. However, the number of postcards so produced over the years is incalculable, and in recent years, many have found their way into circulation.

Opposite above: Lady Ismay, 1911.

Opposite below: Westward Ho, 11 June 1914.

Left: A page from *The Bristol Channel & District Guide* of 1914, showing an advertisement for one of the major Ilfracombe photographers, Mr Batten. He was a most accomplished photographer and much of his work shows passengers aboard the steamers alongside Ilfracombe Pier. Four examples of Mr Batten's work follow.

Below: Cambria, 12 July 1911.

Right: George Owen, following in his father's footsteps, became a master tailor in his home town of Swansea. In 1965, the demand for his kind of tailoring having dwindled, George sold the business and went to sea as an ordinary seaman, eventually reaching the rank of quartermaster with P. & O. He is seen here in the late 1970s, serving aboard the *Canberra*.

Opposite above: Devonia, 23 June 1932.

Opposite below: Occasionally Mr Batten would photograph passengers on the pier. This example, dated 23 August 1928, is of interest as it shows the young Herbert George Owen, in the centre with the raincoat over his arm, standing on the right of his sister, Marjorie. The late Mr Owen was considered to be the *doyen* of Bristol Channel steamer historians and became a very good friend.

At the end of the 1954 season, which marked the culmination of five successive summers of appalling weather, P. & A. Campbell Ltd found itself in serious financial difficulties. A management committee was formed to address the problems of falling passenger figures. Among the measures instituted were the appointment of a publicity manager, who suggested that on-board music and entertainment might attract the public. A wide variety of artists were engaged, including the young Shirley Bassey who, in the mid-1950s, was beginning to gain a foothold on her glittering singing career. The following photographs show some of the artists who became regular performers on the 'Showboats', as they were called, during the mid-1950s.

Opposite: Shirley Bassey on the bridge of the *Bristol Queen* at Ilfracombe in 1955.

Above: The 'pin-up' personality Sabrina (centre), accompanied by actress Susan Irvin, being greeted by the Chairman of Ilfracombe Council, Mrs Cicely Norman, after disembarking from the *Glen Usk* at Ilfracombe.

Right: Singer June Palmer, a regular performer on the steamers during the 1950s.

June Palmer, with Capt. George Gunn, on the bridge of the *Cardiff Queen*.

Right: Singer and guitarist Peter Ricardo and his partner, 'Exotic Dancer' Jobyna.

Below: The Malayan Police Pipe and Drum Band could always be counted on to give a stirring performance. Not only did they perform on the steamers, but would also disembark at Ilfracombe and give a display on the pier.

Other forms of entertainment were also provided, such as this fashion show given by four models from Samuel Hall of Cardiff aboard the *Bristol Queen* on the Whit Sunday 'Showboat' in 1955.

Opposite above: The White Funnel Players aboard the *Glen Usk,* with singer Margaret Cotter at the microphone.

Opposite below: Margaret Cotter was not only a singer. She was described in the local press as a 'Singing Hostess'. Her other duty was to act as a stewardess, dispensing drinks to the passengers on deck. She is seen here with two of her colleagues aboard the *Glen Usk* in 1955.

Among the other 'personalities' of the Bristol Channel were the steamer enthusiasts – that band of hardy souls who were, and still are, to be seen on board, complete with cameras and binoculars, day in, day out, whatever the weather. Here, the 'hardcore' of Bristol Channel regulars are seen enjoying an evening cruise from Cardiff to Weston aboard the *Glen Usk* on Wednesday 11 May 1955. They are, from left to right, the late Gerald Phillips, the late Miss Olwen James, (unknown), John Reypert, Donald Anderson, Norman Bird, (unknown), Viv Davies and the late Joe Searle. (John Brown)

Opposite above: The younger generation was also provided for with jazz and rock 'n' roll cruises, one of which is in full swing aboard the *Britannia* in 1956.

This photograph shows, on the left, Mr H.A. Allen, who for many years lived in Sussex and was a much-respected authority on the South Coast steamers. With his notebook and pen in his hand he is undoubtedly recording the timings of the trip. On the right, with binoculars at the ready, is Mr Ernest Nurse of Bristol, an authority on UK excursion steamers in general. They are seen aboard the *Bristol Queen* during the 1950s.

On the bridge of the *Glen Gower,* off Penarth Head in July 1957. On the left is Capt. Leo Virgo and on the right is Chief Officer David Miles, both long-serving Campbell personnel. The lady on the wheel is Miss Florence Chadwick, who had arrived in Weston-super-Mare with the intention of breaking the record for swimming the Bristol Channel from Weston to Penarth, the existing record then being eight hours and twenty-nine minutes. Her first attempt, on Monday 22 July 1957, had to be postponed owing to rough weather, but the *Western Mail* later reported:

> As dusk fell on Sunday 3 August, Florence Chadwick, the thirty-six-year-old American swimmer, and holder of nine world records, plunged into the muddy waters of the Bristol Channel at Anchor Head, Weston-super-Mare. She entered the water at 9.15 p.m. to the cheers of thousands of holidaymakers and a civic send off from the Mayor of Weston. Accompanying her on the crossing was a boat carrying nine officials, including three observers… Miss Chadwick completed her attempt when she reached Penarth Head at 3.22 p.m. on the following morning, thus setting a new record of six hours and seven minutes.

Miss Chadwick stated that she made the steamer crossing in order to familiarise herself with the local landmarks and navigational lights, and added that Capt. Virgo and Chief Officer Miles were of great assistance to her.

seven

To Boulogne with the
Glen Gower

The *Glen Gower's* last visit to Boulogne before the Second World War broke out took place on Sunday 27 August 1939. She was scheduled to call there again the following Tuesday, but the crossing was cancelled owing to the 'International situation', as Capt. William Bruford recorded in the log book. (The last pre-war visit to Boulogne was made by the *Brighton Queen* on Monday 28 August 1939.)

Immediately after the war Government restrictions effectively prohibited day trips to the Continent. These restrictions were particularly irksome to P. & A. Campbell and the General Steam Navigation Co. of London, both of whom pressed the Government to allow the resumption of such sailings. A partial relaxation came into force in 1954, which allowed both companies to sail to the Continent on condition that passengers carried full passports, that no duty-free or tax-free concessions would be allowed, and that the maximum amount of sterling that could be taken out of the UK was to be £5. A further restriction was placed upon the White Funnel steamers, in that sailings were to start and end at Newhaven and that no *en route* calls at the piers at Brighton, Eastbourne or Hastings were allowed. The company continued to press for no-passport trips from the Sussex resorts but, in the meantime, arranged for ten-day trips to be made to Boulogne.

Unfortunately, the summer of 1954 was one of appalling weather with much rain and frequent gales. The *Glen Gower's* first crossing, scheduled for Wednesday 14 July, was cancelled owing to a gale, but she was successful a week later on 21 July. She sailed from the Railway Wharf at Newhaven with a mere 103 passengers and arrived off Boulogne at 2.40 p.m. to find that the port was closed. A bucket dredger had picked up a magnetic mine in the harbour and, along with other shipping, she had to anchor offshore while it was disposed of. She eventually arrived at her berth at 5 p.m., allowing her passengers only an hour ashore.

Of the ten scheduled trips one was cancelled owing to insufficient crew and three were lost because of adverse weather. The four which took place were so poorly patronised, carrying an average of only 135 passengers per trip, that the final two crossings were cancelled in advance. The experience showed that the average holidaymaker did not favour having to travel to a commercial port to make a day trip and certainly did not go away armed with a passport – facts which strengthened the company's continuing negotiations.

The efforts of P. & A. Campbell and the GSN reached a satisfactory conclusion in May 1955, when the British and French Governments agreed that no-passport day trips were to be allowed from Southend, Gravesend, Folkestone, Eastbourne and Newhaven. (It was a most ironic twist of fate that these trips were to be allowed shortly after the sale of the *Empress Queen*, the steamer specifically built for the purpose). Passengers were required to provide three passport-sized photographs and to complete a four-part card, issued by the companies on the day of sailing, bearing prescribed particulars. A share of good fortune was long overdue and this came in 1955, not only with the resumption of no-passport sailings, but in the best possible form – the summer of 1955 proved to have some of the best weather of the 1950s. The *Glen Gower* entered service on Good Friday, 8 April, and after running a variety of trips in the Bristol Channel was laid up again in Bristol from the following Thursday until re-entering service, for her main summer season, on Saturday 21 May.

A poster advertising the resumption of no-passport sailings to France.

Left: Capt. Jack Harris aboard the *Glen Gower* in the Cumberland Basin, Bristol, in May 1955. A photograph which appeared in the Bristol newspapers publicising the resumption of the no-passport sailings.

Capt. Harris was already an experienced coasting master before joining P. & A. Campbell in 1950. During that and the following season he was chief officer of the *Glen Gower* and, in 1952 and 1953, chief officer of the *Cardiff Queen*. He took command of the *Glen Gower* from July 1954 until the end of the 1956 season, and as such, took the *Glen Gower* on most of her Boulogne sailings. He had a reputation for pressing on whatever the weather. Donald Anderson, in his foreword to my book *White Funnels*, wrote, 'Jack Harris, like a bat out of hell, set his course in a straight line, rang down "Full ahead" and flinched not an eyebrow until his destination was achieved.'

A friend and correspondent, Alan Wakeman, served as an ordinary seaman aboard the *Glen Gower* in 1955. He has given me a fascinating account of the ship's early days during that season and I wish to express my gratitude and appreciation to him for allowing me to reproduce his reminiscences here:

We began running a variety of trips in the Bristol Channel, mainly from Cardiff, on Good Friday, 8 April. After mooring up for the night at the Pier Head our first stop was usually the Big Windsor pub for a few drinks, then up Bute Street for a look around, usually finishing up at Sam On Yen's restaurant for a late supper. This was my first experience of Chinese food at a time when the Chinese communities were running laundries instead of restaurants and takeaways. Unlike today there was a limited Chinese menu which consisted of chop suey (2s 6d), chow mein (3s), and fried rice (3s 3d).

I also remember my first experience of rock 'n roll when we ended up in one of the Bute Street clubs where they were playing and jiving to Bill Haley's *Rock Around the Clock*.

On Monday 20 June we left Cardiff at 9.45 p.m. for the south coast, where we were to be based for the main part of the season. We had a good run around and arrived in Newhaven, after a call at Brighton, at about 5 p.m. on the following day.

Thursday 23 June I remember very well as it was not only our first day in service 'down south' but also our first no-passport trip to Boulogne. We swung, with the aid of the harbour tug, *Tidworth*, made fast to the Railway Wharf and left at 9.30 a.m., arriving alongside Eastbourne Pier at 10.30 a.m.

Opposite below: The children have boarded the *Glen Gower* and are having their identity cards checked and stamped.

Above: Eastbourne Pier on Thursday 23 June 1955, shortly before the departure of the *Glen Gower.* These photographs were originally published in the comic *Mickey Mouse Weekly.* The three children are members of the Mickey Mouse Club and prizewinners of one of the comic's competitions. They are being issued with their identity cards prior to boarding. The lady at the middle table is Mrs Elsie Tanner and on her left, partially hidden, is her husband. The couple ran the Eastbourne booking office for many years.

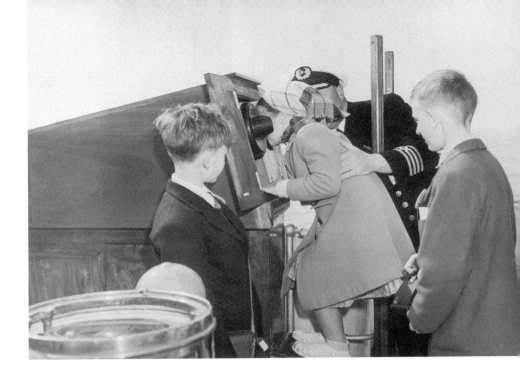

Above and below: As part of their prize the children were also treated to a visit to the bridge, where Ca
Harris showed them the radar, as well as a tour of the engine room with the chief engineer.

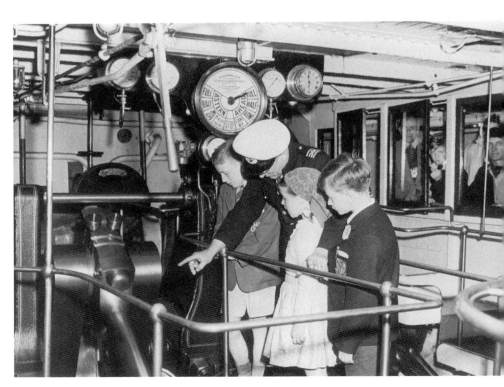

I have been unable to identify the people in this photograph, taken on Eastbourne Pier on 23 June 1955, but they are admiring a commemorative cake sent from Boulogne. The inscription reads 'Hands across the sea. Best wishes to Great Britain from France.'

To continue Alan Wakeman's reminiscences of 23 June:

On 23 June we left Eastbourne Pier a bit late, at 11.10 a.m., owing to the 'festivities', on a course of SE by E six miles out to the *Royal Sovereign* Lightvessel, which I had heard about from my father who was Mate on the *Brighton Belle* before the war. As we steamed past the lightship the passengers had a wave from her crew, the log was set and we altered course to E by S up channel to Boulogne. We were abeam the Boulogne outer breakwater at 2.45 p.m. and moored alongside at 3 p.m. At 4.p.m., after all the harbourside arrival festivities, we swung ship with the aid of the harbour tug *Somme*.

We left Boulogne at just after 7 p.m. and arrived at Eastbourne at 11 p.m., departing twenty minutes later for Newhaven. By the time we arrived at Newhaven it was 12.40 on Friday morning after a day's run of 119 miles. Then, as we were bunkering, we didn't get much sleep before the coaling gang finished at about 3 a.m. owing to the steam crane working on the wharf, swinging bags of coal aboard and the coal clattering down the chutes into the bunkers.

In the morning when we turned to for another Boulogne trip, most of the crew were really shattered, I know I was! This trip was a repeat of Thursday's except that we ran even later and by the time we got back to Newhaven it was nearly two o'clock in the morning. However we did manage to have a bit of a rest on the Saturday which turned out to be the usual off-service day. We didn't get away that easily though as our day off did not start until after we had our first boat and fire drill in Newhaven. As a side issue, on Saturday off-service days, when there was a 'potato boat' from the Channel Islands in the harbour, any crew who wanted to could sign on as casual labourers and earn a bit of extra money helping to unload the new potatoes.

The usual schedule for the Boulogne trip was a four hour crossing, leaving Eastbourne at 10.00. The passengers had four hours ashore until we left at 18.00, scheduled to arrive back at Eastbourne at 22.00. If we didn't get back on time it was usually owing to the wind getting up in the afternoon and having to punch directly into a heavy westerly sea. The course coming back was nearly due west and the Glen Gower didn't like taking it on the bow and couldn't maintain her service speed. Good sea boat that she was, she plodded along pitching and rolling heavily, much to the consternation of the majority of the passengers who were quite seasick, especially after the cream cakes and brandy that were on offer in Boulogne. I remember some crossings taking us nearly six hours, not getting back until midnight, when all the passengers who were already feeling wretched enough then had to queue on the pier to go through customs before they could go home.

Ship Ahoy, the magazine of the South Wales branch of the World Ship Society, published a brief article by two of its members who were aboard on 23 June, which included the following:

The trip was fully booked with 562 passengers, which promises well for the remaining trips this season. The press was well represented on board as were the BBC and news cameramen. The weather being ideal and the catering of a high standard, all had a most enjoyable day, although Boulogne itself still grimly reminds us of the ravages of war. There was cabaret and other entertainment on board and, thanks to the excellent office organisation, embarkation and disembarkation problems were reduced to a minimum.

In his annual statement to shareholders the Chairman of P. & A. Campbell Ltd stated that the cross-Channel sailings during the glorious summer of 1955 had been an unqualified success and that, as a result, the no-passport facilities would, in 1956, be available from Brighton, Eastbourne and Hastings, as in the pre-war years.

In the stokehold of the *Glen Gower.*

Aboard *Glen Gower* crossing the English Channel on Friday 24 June 1955. Capt. Harris can be seen on the starboard bridge wing, and the French coast is just coming into sight on the horizon. (John Brown)

Glen Gower at Boulogne in 1956.

Unfortunately, the summer of 1956 was the opposite of that of 1955. The *Glen Gower* lost the equivalent of about four weeks' sailings, partly because of boiler trouble, but mainly because of the appalling weather. The Boulogne trips were particularly badly affected, with 12,000 passengers being carried from four ports with twelve cancellations, as against 16,000 from two ports with no cancellations in 1955. The *Glen Gower* returned to Bristol in September. Never again would a White Funnel paddle steamer cross the English Channel to France.

If you are interested in purchasing other books published by Tempus,
or in case you have difficulty finding any Tempus books in your local bookshop,
you can also place orders directly through our website

www.thehistorypress.co.uk